KU-093-699

Are you an early bird or a night owl?

CURIOUS
Questions &
answers about...
Animals

What's your favourite colour?

Do you like warm weather better, or snow?

If you could eat one food every day what would it be?

If you could have any animal for a pet, which would you choose?

What's your FAVOURITE animal?

Words by Camilla de la Bédoyère

illustrations by Pauline Reeves

Miles Kelly

What is an animal?

Animals are living things that do all of these things...

① Have babies

All animals can make new life like themselves – this is called **having babies**, or **reproduction**.

② Breathe

Animals **breathe** to take air into their bodies. The body needs a gas in the air called oxygen to keep working.

③ Use senses

An animal uses the **senses** of touch, taste, smell, sight and hearing to find out what is going on around it.

Those leaves look tasty!

④ Move

Most animals **move** to get to food and water, to find safe places, and to escape from danger.

> I learnt to stand up 30 minutes after I was born. How old were you when you learnt to stand?

⑤ Eat

Animals must **eat** food to stay alive. Food gives them energy so they can **move** and **grow**.

Munch!

⑥ Get rid of waste

Waste is leftover food that an animal's body doesn't need.

> Waste not want not! Dung beetles like me use elephant poo for lots of things!

⑦ Grow

All animals start small and **grow** bigger until they are old enough to **have babies** of their own.

Why do crocodiles eat stones?

Because they swallow their meaty meals whole, and the stones help to grind up the food in their tummies!

> Crocs are one of the world's biggest carnivores, or meat-eaters. We eat fish, birds, rats, snakes, lizards and even deer and pigs.

What makes flamingos pink?

Flamingos are pink because they eat pink shrimps that live in VERY salty lakes! They feed with their heads upside down.

> Can you see any other upside-down eaters around here?

Who likes eating greens?

Leaves and other greens taste great to herbivores (plant-eaters) like sloths. Some greens are tough to eat, so they spend lots of time chewing.

Anteaters like me eat ants and termites — thousands of them every day! We lick them up with our long, sticky tongues.

Are animals picky eaters?

They can be! Some only eat one special food. Others, like tiger sharks and brown bears, will eat almost anything they can find!

What are senses?

Senses are the body's way of finding out about the world. Animals use senses to locate food, find their way about, avoid danger and make friends. The five main senses are **hearing**, **sight**, **smell**, **taste** and **touch**.

HEARING

Ear

Do bugs have ears?

Yes – lots of bugs can hear better than humans, but our ears can be in strange places! I'm a bush cricket, and my ears are on my legs.

TOUCH

What are whiskers for?

A cat's whiskers are super-sensitive. I use them to feel things – they can tell me if a space I want to crawl into is too small for my body.

How do snakes smell?
Snakes can smell with their tongues. They flick them in the air to detect any appealing pongs!

SMELL

TASTE

Why is it a bad idea to lick a frog?

I make a foul-tasting slime in my skin. It stops animals from eating me.

SIGHT

Do all animals have two eyes?
Some animals have more than two! Most spiders have eight eyes but cave spiders have none. They live in caves where it's always dark.

Did you know?

A **fulmar** is a foul seabird. It spits a stinky oil at anyone who gets too close.

The **giraffe** is the tallest animal that lives on land.

Lobsters have blue blood and some dogs have blue tongues.

When a **sandtiger shark** wants to sink to the sea bed, it has to burp first!

A spiny **sea urchin** is covered in tiny feet. Its mouth is on its bottom!

Mimic octopuses can change shape and colour. They can pretend to be fish or sea snakes.

Sweat bees like the smell and taste of human sweat!

If a **sponge** is broken into bits, this strange sea creature is able to put itself back together again.

The **dung beetle** is the strongest animal on Earth. If it were the size of a human it could pull six buses full of people!

A **spider** eats about 2000 bugs a year.

Australian **burrowing frogs** cover themselves in slime, so when flies land on them they get stuck – and the frogs can gobble them up.

Bees waggle their bottoms in a crazy dance to tell each other where to find the best flowers.

Hippos don't just yawn when they are tired – they also yawn when they are angry or scared.

A **blue whale** eats millions of pink shrimps, so its poo is pink too. Each poo can be bigger than you!

A **catfish** can use its whole body to taste. Its skin is covered with taste buds.

What's inside an animal?

If you had to build an animal from scratch, here's what you would need...

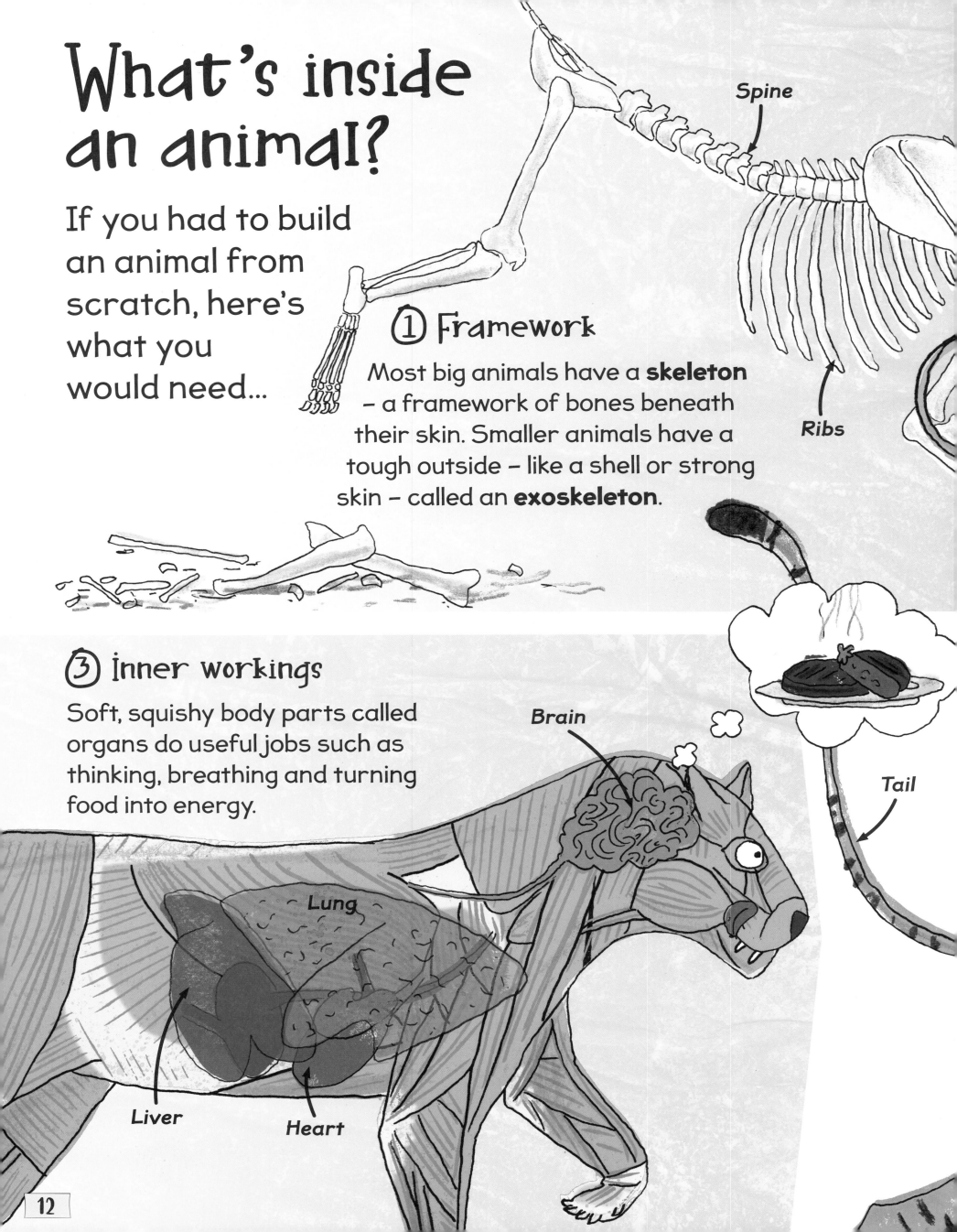

Spine

Ribs

① Framework

Most big animals have a **skeleton** – a framework of bones beneath their skin. Smaller animals have a tough outside – like a shell or strong skin – called an **exoskeleton**.

③ Inner workings

Soft, squishy body parts called organs do useful jobs such as thinking, breathing and turning food into energy.

Brain

Tail

Lung

Liver

Heart

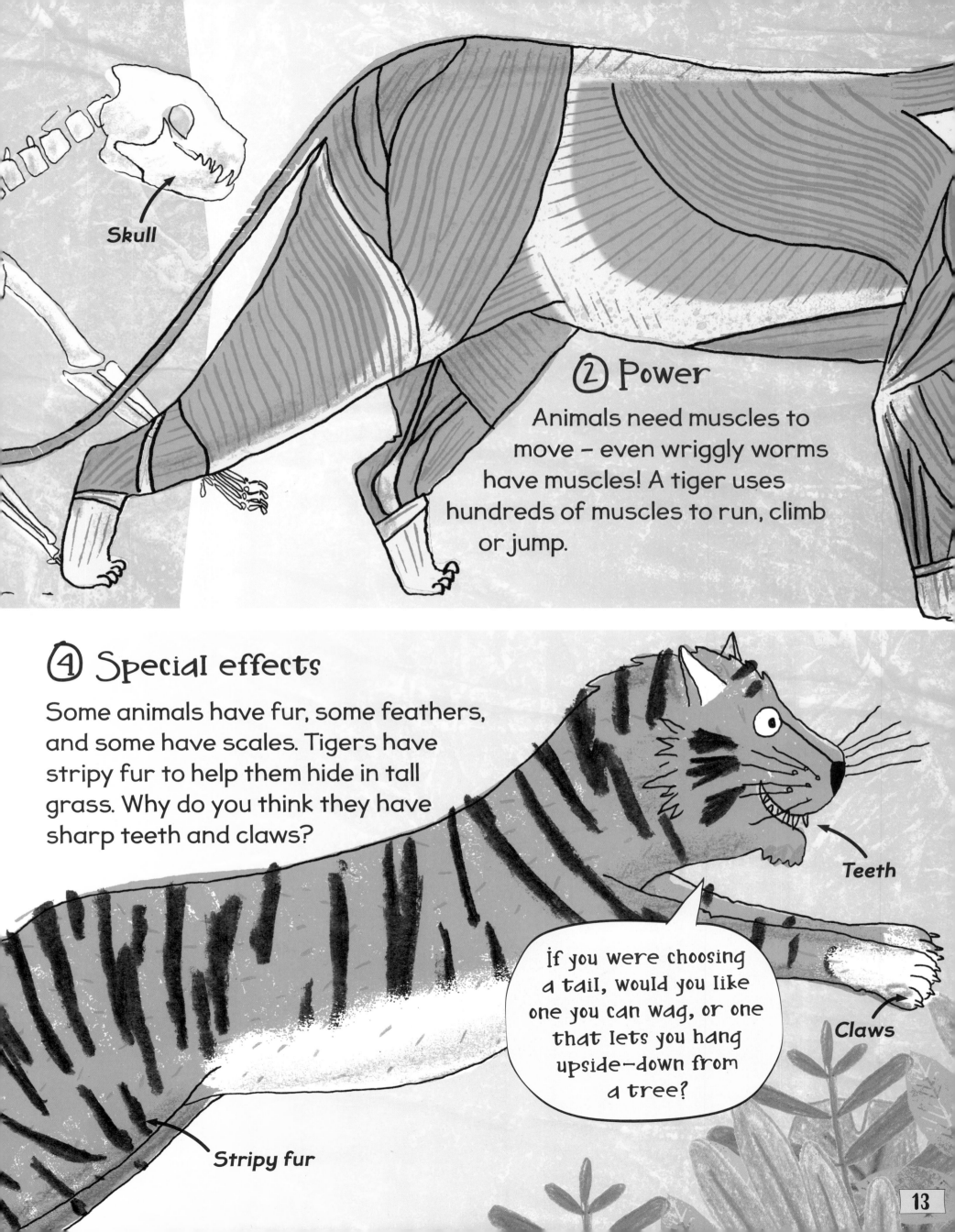

Skull

② Power

Animals need muscles to move – even wriggly worms have muscles! A tiger uses hundreds of muscles to run, climb or jump.

④ Special effects

Some animals have fur, some feathers, and some have scales. Tigers have stripy fur to help them hide in tall grass. Why do you think they have sharp teeth and claws?

Teeth

If you were choosing a tail, would you like one you can wag, or one that lets you hang upside-down from a tree?

Claws

Stripy fur

Why are you blue?

Colours and patterns make an animal beautiful! They can also make an animal look scary, or help it to hide.

Blue-ringed octopus

My colour is a sign of danger. When I'm scared, blue circles appear on my skin. They are a warning that I can kill any attackers with venom.

Blue morpho butterfly

Danger or disguise?

Some animals blend into the background. This is called camouflage. Others have colours and patterns that warn enemies to stay away. Which of these creatures are using camouflage, and which are using warning colours?

Strawberry poison dart frog

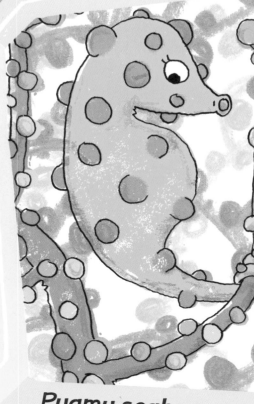

Pygmy seahorse

Blue shark

My colours help me hide. A blue or dark grey shark can prowl through the sea, unseen by the fish it is looking for.

Would you rather have blue feet, like me, or a blue bum, like a baboon?

Blue-footed booby

Southern crowned-pigeon

My beautiful blue feathers make me look healthy and fit to attract a mate.

Leaf insect

Banded sea krait

Lion

Would you rather?

Winter is coming! Would you prefer to travel to somewhere warm, like a **sand martin**, or curl up and sleep through it, like a **dormouse**?

ZZZzz...

Would you rather be spotted like a **leopard**, or striped like a **tiger**?

Is it better to have a long neck, like a **giraffe**...

...or lots of arms like an **octopus**?

You look soooo cute!

A giraffe uses its long neck to reach leaves in tall trees. An octopus uses its arms to move, touch, taste and gather food.

If you were an animal baby would you prefer to sit in dad's pouch, like a **seahorse**, or in mum's, like a **kangaroo**?

It's picnic time! Would you prefer to tuck into a rotting dead animal like a **vulture**, or suck down some animal poo like a **sea cucumber**?

Erm... yummy?

Would you rather have armour like a **pangolin**, or spikes like a **pufferfish**?

WHOOSH!

Would you rather be able to dive through the air at 200 kilometres an hour like a **peregrine falcon**, or fly 15,000 kilometres in a single journey like an **albatross**?

Is it better to be best friends with a **shark** or a **crocodile**?

Sharks and crocodiles are both big carnivores. That means they eat other animals, so it's probably not a good idea to try to make friends with either!

Will you play with me?

Why do spiders do cartwheels?

TUMBLE

Desert spiders that have to get across hot sand do cartwheels so their feet don't get burnt!

How high can you jump?

BOUNCE

LEAP

Kangaroos can jump up to 3 metres into the air, but we can't walk, or move backwards.

Why do orang-utans have long arms?

Long arms are great for swinging through trees. We also have hands for gripping branches and grabbing fruit.

SWING

Antelopes leap several metres at a time, springing up in the air to escape from danger.

Which bird flies, but goes nowhere?

HOVER

A hummingbird does. It flaps and twists its wings so that it can hover in front of a flower, where it drinks the sweet nectar.

I can leap more than 100 times my own height.

SPRING

Fleas jump so they can leap from animal to animal, where they suck blood!

19

How fast do cheetahs sprint?

A cheetah is the fastest running animal on the planet. It can reach top speeds of up to 100 kilometres an hour.

① Built for speed

A cheetah's body is packed with small but powerful muscles.

Why do cheetahs run fast?

Like many hunters, cheetahs turn on the speed when they want to catch their lunch! The antelope they chase need to be fast too, if they hope to escape.

Why are tortoises so slow?

Tortoises plod along slowly because they don't need speed to catch their lunch – they eat grass! They don't need to be fast to escape from danger either because their tough shells protect them like a suit of armour.

② Big strides
It has a super-bendy spine and long, slim legs.

③ Long leap
All four of a cheetah's feet leave the ground as it runs.

Why do crabs run sideways?
Because the way their legs bend means they can't run forwards!

Who's playing statues?
During the day, a potoo bird doesn't move at all! It pretends to be a branch. At night, it flies about, hunting bugs to eat.

How many?

An octopus has **3** hearts but an earthworm has **5**.

A squid has **2** tentacles... ... and it has **8** arms.

Sea otters have **800 million** hairs on their bodies.

Tree kangaroos can jump **30** metres from a tree to the ground below.

A snow leopard can leap more than **10** metres in a single bound.

A snake can live for up to **6** months without eating.

A giraffe's tongue is **45** centimetres long.

20 The number of hours three-toed sloths, koalas and lions might sleep in one day.

500,000

The number of kilometres a sooty tern can fly without stopping for a rest.

Monarch butterflies can go on incredible journeys – one butterfly flew more than **4000** kilometres to lay its eggs!

4

The number of wings a bee has.

1

The number of hours it takes a snail to slime its way along just **1** metre of ground.

The largest number of legs ever counted on a millipede.

750

A mother cane toad can lay **35,000** eggs at a time.

36 The length, in centimetres, of the longest insect – a type of stick insect called Chan's megastick.

Is anyone at home?

Yes! An animal home's is a safe place where it can look after its babies. Animal homes are called habitats. They can be as big as an ocean or as small as a single leaf.

Froghopper nest

Who lives in a home made of spit?

Young froghopper insects build a home of froth around themselves! This 'spit' keeps them safe while they grow.

Why do frogs like water?

Because they need to lay their eggs in it. They are amphibians, which means they can live in water or on land.

Some animals that live in or near water have to come up to the surface to breathe air.

Others have gills and breathe underwater.

Frogs like to live in wet places

Birds nest in tree branches

Owls and their chicks live in tree holes

Why do owls hoot?

They hoot to tell other owls to stay away from their tree. Some animals don't like neighbours!

This fox den is under the tree's roots

Ladybirds also lay their eggs on leaves

Would you rather live in a treetop nest with chicks, or in an underground sett with badger cubs?

Can animals make things?

Yes, some animals are expert builders and can make super structures.

① *A hoop of grass...*

② *...turns into a ball...*

③ *...and then a home.*

Which bird builds the best nest?

A dad weaver bird makes his nest by stitching blades of grass together, then stuffing feathers inside to make a soft bed. He sings to tell mum she can lay her eggs there.

① **Strong silk makes the frame**

Why do spiders build webs?

So they can trap flies. A spider makes the silk in its body and then spins it into a web.

② **Sticky silk is used in the spiral**

Who loves mud?

Millions of termites do! They build their huge towering homes from mud. A group of termites that live together is called a colony, and their home can last for years.

There are passages, tunnels, and places to store food inside

A termite mound can be more than 2 metres high!

HOME SWEET HOME

A single queen lays all the eggs